POCKET IMAGES

Cheltenham
at War

The Nelson indicator. This indicator, which was proudly displayed on the front of the Municipal Offices in the Promenade, was erected in November 1941 to correspond with Warship Week—to raise funds in the town towards the manufacturing costs of a warship. Fund-raising for the war effort was a major part of life in Cheltenham; at various times there were Tank Weeks and the long-standing Hurricane Fund.

POCKET IMAGES

Cheltenham at War

Peter Gill

NONSUCH

Promenade water tank. Photographed shortly before it was filled, this was an extra supply of water in case of incendiary bomb raids on the town.

First published 1994
This new pocket edition 2007
Images unchanged from first edition

Nonsuch Publishing
Cirencester Road, Chalford
Stroud, Gloucestershire, GL6 8PE
www.nonsuch-publishing.com

Nonsuch Publishing is an imprint of NPI Media Group

British Library Cataloguing in Publication Data.
A catalogue record for this book is available from the British Library.

ISBN 978-1-84588-410-9

Typesetting and origination by NPI Media Group
Printed in Great Britain

Contents

Introduction

'This morning the British Ambassador in Berlin handed the German Government a final note stating that unless we heard from them by 11 o'clock that they were prepared at once to withdraw their troops from Poland, a state of war would exist between us. I have to tell you now that no such undertaking has been received and consequently this country is at war with Germany.'

Neville Chamberlain, British Prime Minister, 3 September 1939.

Before the war had even been declared Cheltenham had, like the rest of the country, been bracing itself for the possibility. Although a few had actually arrived, evacuees from London and Birmingham had been planned for. Gas masks had already begun to be delivered and the major schools had been advised that their premises might be requisitioned, and that they ought to organize possible alternative accommodation.

When war was declared Cheltenham responded spontaneously. Sport of most natures was immediately cancelled until further notice, theatres and cinemas were closed and volunteers swarmed to join the ranks of servicemen, air raid patrols, local defence volunteers and the various women's volunteer organizations.

As time went on and the people of Cheltenham got used to the idea of being at war things relaxed somewhat. For example, football matches resumed fairly quickly; initially this started with friendly matches for the local teams and then, as the importance of keeping up morale was realized, competitive fixtures were organized. Theatres and cinemas reopened and a form of normality was resumed.

Cheltenham at war was a very different town from the one before the war and hugely different from the one of today. Before hostilities broke out in Europe, Cheltenham was still very much a town steeped in Victorian values and traditions; it prided itself on its spa town status. A policeman would patrol the promenade to ensure that no improperly dressed persons were allowed access; this part of Cheltenham was strictly reserved for the middle and upper classes and the respectable visitors to the town. Industry on a large scale, although in the making, was still not much in evidence, and was very much on the peripheries of the town. The war changed a little of the look of the town and much of the character. Like all towns and villages in Britain Cheltenham served the country proudly and committedly, suffering silently the ordeals and hardships it had to endure.

When people were asked to open their homes to children from Birmingham and London and other high risk areas, they did so without complaints. Furthermore they showed spirit and patriotism equal to any other town. When the call to Dig for Victory went out, it was heard and acted upon: back gardens were dug up and planted, playing fields like those on St Mark's Estate were ploughed up, and students were sent out on half and even full days to help local farmers.

Paper salvage drive. The recycling of household waste was very important and was continually promoted. To reiterate the importance of saving and recycling paper there was a salvage drive in January 1942. This paper and cardboard destructor depot was in Arle Road.

The charitable nature of all people was shown in the strongest light: the women's volunteer services collected and distributed books to the troops stationed nearby, held knitting parties to make clothes for the troops abroad and ensured that those children evacuated to the town had some form of excitement when they organized parties and concerts for them.

The Local Defence Volunteers, which became the Home Guard, was never short of manpower and was given great commitment from its members, whether it was for the night-long guard duties at the Rotunda in Montpellier, which was an ammunition store, or for the mock invasion exercise that took place around the town.

Many of the schools had to shoulder the burden of war. The two grammar schools took in the pupils and teachers of Birmingham grammar schools. The Ladies' and Gentlemen's Colleges had their premises requisitioned by war ministries, which resulted in huge upheavals and reorganization for both pupils and staff.

Everyone was affected by the influx of foreigners to the town. The problem was probably not so much the nationalities as the numbers; from time to time Cheltenham played host to Polish airmen, Norwegian fishermen, New Zealand timbermen, Italian prisoners of war and of course American GIs.

The Americans were the biggest upset to Cheltenham life. With their sweets and comics they charmed the youngsters; with their charm and confidence they bewitched the girls. They took over the Queen's Hotel as an army hospital and infiltrated the local dances. For a great part they were harmless, vociferous visitors, who were allowed into the town on different days depending on the colour of their skin. On one occasion, though, a young girl was raped by two servicemen in Bishops Cleeve; the two guilty parties were sentenced to death by an army court for their actions.

Many Cheltonians were sent to play their part in the war on foreign soils. Some were detailed to the Middle and Far East, some went to Europe; some were caught up in fighting, others were fortunate enough to miss it. Needless to say, however, many men and women from the town lost their lives; many more were wounded.

Cheltenham didn't suffer the kind of air raid attacks of somof the bigger more industrial towns, but it was bombed particularly badly on two occasions. Lives and property were lost on the nights of 11/12 December 1940 and 27 July 1942: people were suddenly homeless and had to learn to cope with a more direct consequence of war.

When all have to suffer equally the deaths of friends and relatives, the destruction of property, the trials of rationing and the great need to help one another, class systems that have been built up over generations are easily broken down. By the end of the war many of the class barriers were gone; people had suffered together and survived together. Service personnel were coming back from abroad with experiences of a wider world and technology was changing the lives of everyone. Cheltenham during the war years was changing its whole character both internally and externally.

Collecting photographic material for this era was never going to be easy. Film was expensive, rationed and in very short supply during the war, and cameras were still quite a luxury item. Then there were certain things that couldn't be photographed for security reason—the military installations, the gun emplacements and (for the general public) the bomb damage. There is a lot that I haven't been able to record because of these restrictions, but any more material that comes to light would still be of great interest to me.

However, I have obtained and put together a collection of photographs that give a glimpse of the life of Cheltenham in the war years 1939–45. Many of the photographs are from private collections; many have not been publicly viewed before. They all tell the same story of a provincial town, similar to many, the memories of which are herein portrayed.

Peter Gill
May 1994

One

Everyday Life

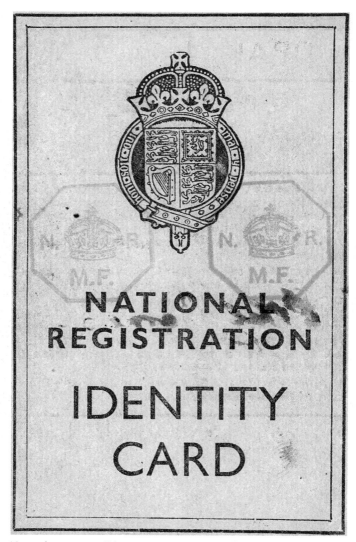

National registration. Of paramount importance to the security of a war-stricken Britain was the ubiquitous identity card. Everyone had to have one, and they had to be carried at all times. This card was registered in 1940, and belonged to Barbara Barnes.

Baby respirators. Midway through February 1940, babies' anti-gas helmets and respirators were being issued and fitted at ARP depots. This baby was fitted at The Elms on the Swindon Road.

Fund-raising. Ten-year-old Jean Smith and her friend eight-year-old Alan Ventura, both of Prestbury Road, held a bazaar in Jean's front garden on Saturday 31 August 1940 to raise money for the Cheltenham Hurricane Fund. They managed to collect in total £4 17s. 9d.

Hurricane Fund. The Mayor of Cheltenham John Howell signed a cheque in the first week of September 1940 for £7,000. The cheque was then sent to Lord Beaverbrook, Minister of Aircraft Production, for the purchase of a Hurricane fighter. On the left of the mayor is Mr E.W. Deacon, the then Borough Treasurer. This was the first Hurricane that Cheltenham had managed to purchase.

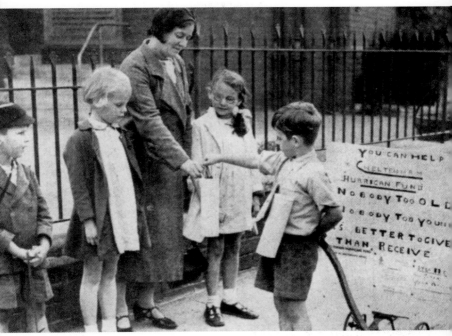

Collecting money. Peter Palmer of Peterville in Exmouth Street made good use of his summer holiday from Naunton Park Junior School. He made a cart and collecting boxes so that he could go out to raise more funds for the Cheltenham Hurricane Fund. This photograph was taken in the last week of August 1940, shortly after he had returned to school.

Penny a Week. Mayor T.W. Waite stands with members of the Red Cross after a meeting with the Red Cross Penny a Week collectors, August 1942. This was yet another fund-raising venture by Cheltenham citizens.

Tank Week. In September 1942 there was a push to raise funds to buy a tank. This campaign was opened by Mayor T.W. Waite in front of the Town Hall.

Warship Week. This was the opening ceremony of Warship Week in November 1941, during which funds were raised towards the purchase of a warship. Note in the background the model of a battleship, which stood in the Promenade during this week.

Dig for Victory exhibition. In April 1942 an exhibition was held in the Town Hall illustrating the many ways in which local people could increase agricultural output. Mayor T.W. Waite, in his chain of office, former mayor John Howell CBE, seated far left front row, and other councillors watch as the exhibition is formerly declared open.

Above: Play your part! An exhibition representative shows how everyone, young and old, rich and poor, could 'play their part'. Emphasis wasn't just given to producing more but also to using less and wasting nothing.

Below: Street Savings. In February 1943 Mayor T.W. Waite presented residents of Chatsworth Drive, Fairfield Avenue and Byron Road with a Street Savings Group banner. This was an acknowledgement by National Savings of the combined efforts of residents of these streets to increase public funds.

Lending to win the war. On Monday 5 February 1940 a Savings Bureau was opened adjoining the post office in the Promenade; simultaneously a National Savings Week was declared. Here Ald. E.L. Ward signs a cheque for £1,000 on behalf of the Cheltenham and Gloucester Building Society to purchase Defence Bonds. People present are, left to right: Mrs K.A. Woodward, Mrs D. Howell, Mrs D.L. Lipson, Mr H. Robertshaw, Mr C. Blount, Ald. E.L. Ward, Mayor John Howell, Mr J.E. McKeon and Councillor G.B. Compton.

Holidays at Home. In August 1942 Mayor T.W. Waite opened a Holidays at Home campaign, intended to encourage people to stay in Cheltenham for their holidays. It promoted leisure opportunities available in the town.

Women's Voluntary Service. Cheltenham members of the WVS are seen here outside their headquarters in Pittville Street in April 1940. Back row, left to right: Mrs W.A. Hollins, Mrs M. Cadell, Miss I. Seton, Miss E. Adlard, Mrs V. Cousland. Front row: Mrs S. Archer, Mrs D.L. Lipson, Miss E.J. Tomkinson (regional organizer), Mrs S. Colchester-Wemyss (county organizer), Mrs V. Boulnois, Mrs G.T. Verry, Miss V. Goss.

Working party. Organized by Mrs Bassett, Mrs Franks and Miss Swanston, the Bishops Cleeve working party met fortnightly at Owl's End, the home of Mrs Bassett and Miss Swanston. Between October 1939 and May 1940 the women knitted and sent to forces abroad 721 garments.

Hawling ladies. In the village of Hawling the ladies organized weekly working parties at the village hall to produce woollen garments for the British troops. Mrs C.P. Prescot of Hawling Manor was the president and Mrs O. Richards the honorary secretary. All the finished articles were sent to the WVS district depot in Cheltenham. The little girl in front is Barbara Mustoe, aged eight, who attended the groups from the start and made many items. This photograph was taken in March 1940.

YMCA Tea Car. In April 1942 a presentation was made by Mrs J.H. Trye, on behalf of the women of Boston, USA, of a YMCA Tea Car to the women of Cheltenham. Mrs Trye is holding the bouquet of flowers.

Field kitchens. In February 1942 the WVS gave a demonstration of army field kitchen cooking in Cheltenham.

First aiders. This photograph, taken in mid-October 1940, shows Cheltenham's First Aid Party members, who were stationed at The Elms on the Swindon Road.

Auxiliary Fire Service volunteers. On Saturday 4 May 1940 a demonstration was given in the Promenade to encourage part-time volunteers for the AFS. Trailer-pumps manned by fire-fighters in full kit were parked outside the post office and firemen were on hand to answer enquiries.

Opposite above: Fire guards. Mayor T.W. Waite presents cups to the winners of the fire-fighting competition in May 1942.

Opposite below: Retiring town clerk. Mayor T.W. Waite presents Mr R.O. Seacombe, the retiring town clerk, with a message of appreciation in November 1941.

On 9 January 1943 Mr W.J. Bache retired from his post as Borough Electrical Engineer, and is seen here receiving a token of appreciation.

Mayor-making day. After the ceremony of mayor-making in November 1942, councillors and former mayors pose for a photograph. Mayor T.W. Waite stands in the centre with the mayoress to the left and his predecessor John Howell CBE, FRCS, to the right.

John Howell CBE, FRCS. Mayor when war broke out, John Howell served Cheltenham as a councillor for many years and was an energetic and enthusiastic mayor for his three-year term, starting in 1938 and ending in 1941.

T. Wilfrid Waite. The successor to John Howell, Mayor Waite continued the good work and was equally energetic, sponsoring many of the fund-raising events held in the town and helping to maintain a good spirit and high morale in Cheltenham.

Leckhampton Juniors football team. On Saturday 7 April 1940 the Leckhampton Juniors beat Whaddon Juniors 6–1 at Leckhampton. Standing, left to right: A.T. Bendall (treasurer), B. Eeles, A. Bailey, J. Selley, J. Brunsdon, W. Scottorn, J. Mitchell, A. Christopher. Seated: P. Townsend, L. Thorndale, E. Critchley (captain), J. Taylor, M. Manton.

Whaddon Juniors football team. The losing team, but still smiling! Standing, left to right: W. Caseley, D. Townley, D.E. Fox, K. Rushworth (referee), M. Hughes, R.L. Fox, E. Aston. Seated: G.H. Ballinger, T. Upton, P. Rushworth (captain), A.W. Walker, T. Wren.

Cheltenham men's hockey team. Pictured is the team that played Pershore on Saturday 24 February at the Victoria Ground in Cheltenham. Standing, left to right: P.R. Strickland, W.K. Wilson, R. Lind, A.F. Fairlie-Clarke, R.E. Yeend, C. Howard. Seated: F.H. Ward, J. Gilbert, A. Fulwell, L.W. Greensted, J.F. Cuss.

Boy boxers. More evidence of the strong sporting activities in wartime Cheltenham is this group of competitors outside the Drill Hall in Cheltenham after the contests for the county boxing championships from the Gloucestershire and Herefordshire boys' clubs. The few that can be identified are: T. Finch, front row second from the right; R. Gill, directly behind; K. Midwinter, at the right shoulder of Finch; J. Ballinger (?), front row third from right; R. Newman, directly behind; D. Midwinter, to the left and peering through the gap.

St Stephen's Church wedding. Further proof that as far as possible life went on as normal are the number of weddings that took place. F.B. Hansford of 7 Orchard Terrace, Libertus Road, married Jean C. Williams of Wellesbourne, Oakfield Street, on Tuesday 6 February 1940.

St Peter's Church, Cleeve Hill. In January 1940 Miss P. Stephens married William Griffin at St Peter's Church. The photograph shows the newly-weds in the centre with their family outside Two Hedges, the house that gave the road in Woodmancote its name.

Two

School Life

Empire Day. In the last week of May 1940 these children of the Gloucester Road Junior School took part in an Empire Pageant to commemorate Empire Day. The Revd G. Douglas-Evans delivered an address to the children earlier in the day.

St John's School. This photograph was taken on the same day as the one above. These pupils of St John's School were addressed by the Borough Education Secretary Mr W.T. Long, who is standing on the right; the lady standing next to him is the headmistress Miss Dallimore. The Revd C.H. Lancaster, the vicar of St John's, is standing on the left.

Miss G.E. Linnett. In April 1940 Miss Linnett, a teacher at Naunton Park School, changed her uncultivated allotment into a productive piece of land, in direct response to the highly publicized Dig for Victory campaign.

Pate's Grammar School for Girls. The new premises for the girls' grammar school in Albert Road opened on Tuesday 19 September 1939. As this picture illustrates the building was far from finished, but had to be opened prematurely to accommodate the evacuated girls from King Edward's High School in Birmingham. Classes were arranged for the Cheltenham girls in the mornings and for the evacuees in the afternoons.

Cheltenham Grammar School. This photograph shows Mayor T. W. Waite outside the Town Hall after the Cheltenham Grammar School Spech Day in May 1942. The boys also had to share their school with Birmingham children—boys from Moseley Grammar School.

Opposite above: Grammar School boys. Voluntary work for boys at the school was greatly encouraged and organized; boys were divided into squads under masters for night-time air-raid duties, serving meals and cleaning, among others. Here volunteers construct a Morrison shelter in August 1941 at the home of Councillor H.C. Grimwade of St Mark's. Four of the councillor's children are inside.

Below: Rugby XV. The Grammar School Rugby XV that lost fourteen points to six to the Cheltenham College 2nd XV on Saturday 16 November 1940. Standing, left to right: K.J. Evans, H.R. Holborrow, C.F. Manger, R.H. Baker, J.S. Jones, D.R. Lewis, T.H. Jones, F. Robson. Seated: R. White, A.W. Workman, J.E. StV.L. Beasley, D.J. Knee (captain), J.H. Gregory, S.W. Smith, V.S. Brett.

Cheltenham Grammar School pupil David Bick, seated far right, is here helping with hay-making in the Lower Orchard, Malvern View, Apperley, in the summer of 1941. The 'tractor' illustrates the fate of many old cars during the war. It is a converted 1928 Morris Cowley with the rear axle bolted on to the chassis, giving the driver a very unsteady ride. The vehicle was known as L2U as this was painted on the number plate. With David Bick are Ted Andrews of Apperley, at the front of the tractor, Hilary Belcher, seated, and David's brother Ewart, standing to the left of David.

Dean Close School masters, summer 1941. This picture shows the staff who kept Dean Close School running through the war years. After the bad economic situation of the 1930s these men agreed to take a reduction in wages in order to keep the school in existence. Most of them were still at the school to celebrate VE-Day in 1945. Back row, left to right: W.R. Thorne, O.P. Masterman-Smith, E.V. Tanner (chaplain), R.M. Thomas, A.W. Golder. Front row: F.G.K. Westcott, F.R.H. Brian, F. Horsley, H. Elder (headmaster), A.H. Warr, C.A.P. Tuckwell, E.S. Hoare.

House prefects. A humorous photograph taken at the end of the war of the Dean Close house prefects in gas masks. The masks were never actually used, and were worn only at times of inspection.

Junior boys. In the first wartime summer of 1940 Dean Close began to offer its services to local farmers. These junior boys had spent the day potato-picking.

Haymaking. At first, farmers had treated the help with a modicum of suspicion, but after the first year the school had more requests for help than it could ultimately cater for.

Farming beet. During half-holidays organized work parties cycled out from the school to the farms, and during summer holidays an annual camp was arranged to serve the needs of half a dozen farmers.

Above: Hay collecting. As the boys became more adept and used to the work they were given greater responsibilities, such as the control of horses and carts.

Left: Time for a break! Even during a long day's work there was time to catch a light-hearted photograph of two senior boys 'taking a swig'.

Opposite above: Earthing up potatoes. Much of the help the school gave was to Mr F.H. Lewis of Copse Green Farm, Elmstone Hardwicke. These boys are bringing potatoes to the surface with a horse-drawn plough.

Opposite below: Tea-break. The workers enjoy a respite from the toil at Copse Green. Among other chores they had been thinning out mangolds.

Left: Kitchen squad. As the war went on finding domestic labour for the school became more and more difficult, and boys had to help in most general domestic activities. Here three members of a kitchen picket peel potatoes. Head of House Harrison is on the left, then Prefect A.H. Knowles-Bolton and finally O.R.A. Stoney, three Gate House seniors in 1942.

Below: Trench-digging. Work wasn't limited to the kitchens and farms. Here boys get involved in digging trenches at Elmstone Hardwicke in response to a fifth columnist scare. Fortunately they were never needed; nor was the training that the boys were given in road-block construction.

Cricket. Despite the war cricket survived, although not in the state it had been before. In the summer of 1940 the 1st XI at Dean Close played the masters. At this time the players still had white flannels to wear—it was before clothes rationing. Masters C.A.P. Tuckwell and E.S. Hoare lead the teams out on to the field.

Dean Close hockey team. In March 1940 the school was still in exile in Monkton Combe—moved out of Cheltenham when the buildings were requisitioned. This team returned on Saturday 9 March to play Oxford University Occasionals at the school ground. Left to right: D.G. Tugwell, A.B. Mills, G.L. Harrison, A.N. Hilltout, A.S.H. Tugwell, N.H. Abraham, T.W. Backhouse, T.J.M. Scott, R.A. Bayliss, P.K. Calder, E.J. Farmer.

John Bell MA. The headmaster of Cheltenham Gentlemen's College from September 1938 until May 1940, John Bell had to oversee and organize the huge upheaval of moving the college lock, stock and barrel to Shrewsbury.

Arriving at Shrewsbury. As soon as war broke out the college was told that it would have to give up its premises for Government offices. Although this eventually turned out to be totally unnecessary the school packed up its belongings and pupils, and in September 1939 moved to Shrewsbury School.

Coming home! After just two terms away from Cheltenham the boys are helping to load the removal trucks as they prepare to come home. It was decided that the college wouldn't be used and that the upheaval had been an alarmist move on the part of the Government.

Even the bikes! Absolutely everything that was deemed reasonably necessary travelled to Shrewsbury and back, including the chief form of transport, the bicycles—here being loaded to return to Cheltenham.

A.G. Elliot-Smith. Taken shortly after the war at a parliamentary debate, and standing second from the left, is A.G. Elliot-Smith, the successor to John Bell as headmaster of the college. He took over in May 1940 and saw the school safely through to the end of the war. Standing on the left is Miss Picton Turbervill, the sometime MP for Wrekin.

Margaret E. Popham. Holding the position of Principal of the Cheltenham Ladies' College from 1937 until 1953, Margaret E. Popham showed great strength of character throughout the war. She was told while on holiday in Jersey on Christmas Day 1938 that in the event of war the college would be displaced and the premises requisitioned, yet with great spirit she held on to parts of the college and kept the focus firmly in Cheltenham.

The swimming pool. When the Office of Works threatened to take the college over Margaret Popham filled the swimming pool with water, correctly thinking that they would not want to requisition it. She kept the knowledge to herself that it could be boarded over, which it subsequently was, giving the college a large hall area. The picture shows the deep end with the diving board intact.

The shallow end. The whole of the 'swimming pool' was filled with desks, chairs, blackboards and other teaching aids. Close by was Christ Church, where the vicar Mr Coursey allowed prayer and scripture classes, and lent the school the parish room for classes.

The marble corridor. Still needing more room, Margaret Popham telephoned the army in Bristol and asked for twenty army huts to be sent immediately to be made into classrooms. She convinced them that it was on the authority of the War Office and the huts were dispatched and erected in a circular pattern. The boarding running to the huts became known as the marble corridor, after the corridor within the college premises.

Library transport. The college library was re-housed partly in The Grange (latterly the home of Cheltenham MP Sir Charles Irving), resulting in the librarian having to move essential books in a baby's pram.

Private study. The swimming pool cubicles were used for private study and for coaching. Margaret Popham even utilized a towel cupboard of the baths as her office at one stage.

Seven Springs House. Many girls had to be moved to various parts of the Cotswolds in September 1939 until the time when Miss Popham arranged for their return and the school moved back to its premises. The junior girls went to Seven Springs House on the Cowley road.

Stratford House. This was one of the temporary houses used in the town itself. Sevenhampton and Brockhampton manors were also used, the girls being bussed into Cheltenham daily, while some girls – the lower first division – had to go to Lilleshall Hall in Shropshire, where they were visited weekly by the principal.

Lauriston House. Another of the Cheltenham houses is shown here. By early 1941 most of the girls and their teachers were back in their rightful places.

Left: A group of trainee teachers at St Paul's College before being called up. After the war students who had been called up were re-admitted to the college to finish off their studies.

Below: Table-tennis team. The St Paul's College table-tennis team of 1944–5. Back row, left to right: G. Marsden, H. Stockton, N. Davidson. Front row: R. Hubble, the Principal, D. Thomas (captain), R. Selwood, D. Kirk.

Three

Industry

A.E. Pulsford and Son. The removal contractors Pulsford and Son used these two vehicles throughout the war. They were also required, however, for more than four days a week to ferry equipment to Newport and Cardiff for Air Ministry and Ministry of Aircraft Production purposes. The bodies were painted blue with cream writing.

Replacement Albion van. In order to obtain this new van (painted cream with blue writing), the company had to go to great pains, having to get letters of recommendation, a licence to purchase and ultimately Ministry approval. The final cost was £569 15s., plus £11 for an electric starter.

Above: The Famous. The Cheltenham tailors and outfitters as it appeared during the war. Note the extra entrance door on the corner of the building.

Below: An interior view of The Famous. For those who had the money and the necessary clothing ration coupons, this is what would have been expected. The shop dated back to 1886, with the Cole family taking over in 1896.

The Famous staff photograph. Taken shortly after the war, this shows for the most part the staff who ran the shop between 1939 and 1945. The superimposed pictures are of brothers Jack (left) and Percy Cole, sons of A.N. Cole, who jointly owned the business. In 1946, when Percy died, Jack was left in sole charge.

Lance-Bombardier J.J. Cole RA. On Saturday 30 December 1939, Jack Cole married Margaret McDougall at Whitefield Memorial Church in Gloucester. Behind the couple is Mr Leslie Slader, who was the best man. Miss Joan McDougall, the bride's sister, was the only bridesmaid. A reception was held at the Connaught Room.

The Gloucestershire Dairy Company Ltd. Some of the staff of the dairy are seen here in the 1930s; most stayed on throughout and after the war. Mary Missen, a long-serving member of the company, is sitting on the right.

Dairy staff in 1937. Back row, left to right: Nelson Hawkins, J.C. Agg, George Young, Harry Williams, J. Smith, Fred Trinder, Harold Piper, Percy Allen, Gordon Grimsford, Victor Gough, Walley Evans, Ernie Fletcher, Cyril Toft, Johnny Street. Front row: 'Jumbo' Pearce, Bill Hayling, J. Johnson, W. Trinder, -?-, Jess Gough, Charles Toft, J. Green.

Butter display. Until food shortages and rationing took its toll the Gloucestershire Dairy Company was producing these wonderful displays made entirely out of butter. The designer was W. Trinder (sitting centre in previous picture). The dairy was the first outside London to pasteurize its milk, which it did in 1932. Subsequently it advertised its milk as 'SAFE' milk.

Milkmen heading for work. A scene familiar at the beginning of the war would have been the milkmen with their ponies and carts starting the day by leaving Imperial Lane.

The 'new' cart. By the end of the war these improved carts were beginning to be used by the dairy; still relying on ponies, they were very much the forerunner of the motorized cart.

H.H. Martyn and Co. This rare interior view of Martyn's Sunningend Works shows Frank Tovey standing in the centre surrounded by the cockpits of Horsa gliders, the type of aircraft that won fame in landing troops at Arnhem and on D-Day. The company also made Mosquito tail units and bomb racks for Wellingtons among other valuable war equipment. This photograph was taken in October 1944.

Sunningend AFC. Made up of workers at Martyn's Sunningend Works, this football team went the whole 1943–4 season unbeaten, winning both the North Gloucestershire Cup and the Cheltenham War League. Back row, left to right: D. Barrett, J. Cannon, R. Gill, A. Gregory, R. Hopkins, R. Holder. Front row: E. Collier, J. Twining, V. Boote, H. Jones (captain), W. Botting, J. Jordan, S. Draper.

Sunningend Sports Club cricket team, seen here on Saturday 25 May 1940. Standing, left to right: B. Ralph, J. Faulkner, F. Bloodworth, S. Evans, G. Jones, A. Sinkinson. Seated: A. Jones, A Faulkner, A. Gregory (captain), P. Greenslade, L. Wheeler.

Gloster Aircraft AFC. With the advent of war a strong link came into being between the Gloster Aircraft Company and H.H. Martyn and Co. This football team, pictured in January 1940, played in the Cheltenham Senior Division. Standing, left to right: M. Loftus, C. Godwin, E. Drew, R. Medcroft, G. Morse, P. Bird, J. Latter. Seated: J. Ryan, A. Millicen, C.H. Cook, F. Redding, G. Crawford.

Smith's Industries. Smith's moved to Bishops Cleeve in May 1940. This is the very first photograph of their new site under construction in the autumn of 1939. It was given the coding CH1 (Cheltenham 1) and was completed in May 1940. The factory was used initially for making special aviation clocks.

Personnel caravan. Parked in the grounds of Cleeve Grange, this is an example of the caravans that housed key personnel of Smith's new factory in 1939–40. Living conditions were quite harsh, with bath and washrooms being set up in the stables of the Grange.

Hotspur gliders. During the war, workers at the Smith's factory became familiar with the Hotspur gliders that used the nearby Stoke Road Aerodrome as a training field.

Camouflage posts, Smith's Industries. Fire personnel are practising in front of the posts which were used to support camouflage cover, seen here at the end of the war. The entire factory was concealed from the air by such cover, and perhaps as a consequence it never suffered a direct hit.

Smith's Fire Brigade personnel. They were photographed with one of their tenders at the end of the war.

The Dowty School of Aircraft Hydraulics, 1942. During the war Dowty's was a great instrument in the British war machine, producing 87,000 undercarriages and nearly a million hydraulic units.

Arle Court staff, 1940. In 1935 George Dowty moved his developing company to Arle Court, where its headquarters remain today. This early staff photograph shows George Dowty, sitting fourth from the right, and R.H. Bound, technical director, third from the left.

Dowty's assembly department. Pictured in March 1940 is the interior of the assembly department at Arle Court. At the peak of wartime activities Dowty's employed 3,000 workers.

Arle Court. Lunch-time outside the staff canteen in March 1940, where hot dinners were provided daily at 8d. per head.

Pressure testing. An engineer is testing the pressure in a hydraulic retracting undercarriage, March 1940.

Fitters at work. These men were working in the engineering shop at Arle Court. Dowty's made parts for many different wartime aircraft, including Hurricane, Typhoon and Whirlwind fighters, Lancaster, Halifax and Blenheim bombers, and Anson and Master trainers.

Female staff. With the men being enlisted, Dowty's like other major employers took on more and more women. At the peak of this trend 50 per cent of all workers at Dowty's were women. This woman is engaged in centre lathe turning.

Bench work. These women are engaged in and training in bench work. Note the poster on the blackboard: during the war propaganda and security posters were everywhere around the factory.

'Last of the Many'. PZ 865, the last of more than 20,000 Hurricane fighters produced during the war that had Dowty hydraulics and tail wheels.

George Dowty. The founder and inspiration of the company is standing beside a test rig for the Lancaster undercarriage. Of the 87,000 Dowty undercarriages built nearly 22,000 were for the Lancaster, and it was regarded by RAF testers as the best undercarriage ever tested for a heavy bomber.

Wartime effort. Even George Dowty had to act as an instructor for this party of visiting RAF personnel.

Visiting personnel. R.H. Bound, second from the left, shows military personnel around the factory. Robert Hunt stands on the far right.

British military personnel. Throughout the war, Dowty's entertained military personnel on inspection tours of the factory and training sessions. These men are inspecting an undercarriage testing rig.

More visitors. It wasn't only in the aircraft industry that Dowty's helped the war effort: ships of the 'Gay Viking' class were also equipped with Dowty hydraulics.

Sir Stafford Cripps. In March 1944 the Minister of Aircraft Production, Sir Stafford Cripps, visited Arle Court. Here he is shown inspecting the Lancaster landing gear test rig. In the foreground is George Dowty, far right; next to him is Sir Stafford, and R.H. Bound is second from the left.

Four

Air Raids

Building shelters. In the first month of war, September 1939, these men are constructing an air raid shelter on the lawns in front of St Paul's Church. There were other shelters at St Paul's Training College and the Royal Crescent Gardens (which held 1,250 people) – and of course many others.

Gas mask drill. In July 1940 the pupils of St Paul's Infant School are seen having a gas mask and air raid drill. They are descending into the shelter that is seen under construction above.

Air raid wardens. A group of volunteer wardens is standing outside a sandbagged shelter in the town. Note their equipment – a small first aid box and a hand water pump.

Suffolk Road bombing. Cheltenham suffered its worst bombing of the war on the night of 11/12 December 1940. The raid started at 7.40 p.m. and lasted until after midnight. An estimated 2,000 incendiary bombs and over 100 high explosives were dropped. This is the bombed house of Mrs W. Iles, who died within.

Above: Dean Close School. Five bombs fell on the school in the same raid. Fortunately the school had dispersed early that year and there were few in residence. However, there were a dozen boys remaining to finish their School Certificate exam.

Left: Junior School classrooms. In the raid all the panes on the south and west sides of the building were broken and the greenhouses were demolished. The dining hall was ankle-deep in fragments of glass and plaster. As these two photographs depict, the main damage was to the Junior School classrooms, which were wrecked.

Crater Pitch. One of the five bombs that fell on the Dean Close premises landed smack in the middle of a hockey pitch, creating a huge crater. Even to this day the pitch is often referred to as Crater Pitch. Master E.S. Hoare stands by.

Victoria Place. The ruins of a cottage property, 12 December 1940. Some six hundred people were made homeless on the night, and newspaper reports stated, unfortunately, that looting of ruined homes had taken place.

Parabola Road, Bayshill. Again in December 1940, more evidence of the bombings: the damage done to a large house in Parabola Road. In total twenty-three people lost their lives that night; almost half of them were residents of Stoneville Street – killed when there was a massive explosion at the nearby railway embankment.

Christ Church area. This shows the crater caused by a bomb landing in the garden of a Christ Church home; the house was only partly damaged. In other areas, the Black and White coach station in St Margaret's Road was destroyed, and the Bristol No. 79 bus was hurled over a wall.

Suffolk Road. Yet more damage to property, again in Suffolk Road. For those that had been killed an emergency mortuary was set up in Waterloo Street.

St Mary's College Hostel. Fortunately when the bomb struck this hostel, Fullwood Hall, part of St Mary's College, the building hadn't been finished and consequently there was no-one in residence. As can be seen there was extensive damage, and the picture shows repair work already under way.

Fullwood Hall. The Principal's house suffered a good deal of spattering when a bomb struck a wall of the building. The building had been bought by the college less than a decade earlier.

Gotherington. On 18 November 1940 the small village of Gotherington suffered a spate of random bombing. Forty-five-year-old Miss Elizabeth Kearsey was killed when a bomb fell just in front of her cottage, causing a fire. The local rector, who was also the Head Special Constable, tried in vain to save her. The picture shows her destroyed home.

Gotherington, 19 November 1940. Another bomb fell very close to Elizabeth Kearsey's house. The scullery and wash-house have been demolished and virtually all the roof tiles have gone. Two evacuee children staying at the house were slightly injured by the bomb.

Five

Those Who Served

Local Defence Volunteers. The Dean Close School contingent of the Local Defence Volunteers, before they were nationally renamed the Home Guard, in the summer of 1940.

Cheltenham territorials. Some of the town's territorials in September 1939, shortly after war had been declared. The territorials were among the first to be called into action by the country.

Smith's Home Guard. In the summer of 1944 Major Eric Desmond, Company Commander, leads H Company Battle Platoon of the Gloucestershire Home Guard from Smith's Industries down the Promenade on a Salute the Soldier Week parade.

Sunningend Home Guard. The men of a platoon probably affiliated to H.H. Martyn and Co. at Sunningend, where many of them worked. The late Richard Gill in the second row, third from the right, used (like other members of the company) a model wooden rifle that had been made in the factory. Had the Germans invaded it wouldn't have been much good unless used as a club! Proper rifles were eventually distributed.

Church parade. In March 1942 members of Cheltenham's Home Guard parade in front of Mayor Waite on their way to St James' Church.

Parade, April 1942. On the occasion of the visit of the Duchess of Gloucester to the Dig for Victory exhibition at the Town Hall, the troops of the Home Guard arranged a special parade.

Territorials. A composite picture of Cheltenham territorials, September 1939. 1. Local officers, left to right: Lieut. C.D. Welford, Lieut. D.G. Howell, Lieut. E.J.F. Rockett, Captain H.G. Mason; 2 and 4. Military Police; 3 and 5. Captain H.G. Mason leads men on the parade ground; 6. Territorials marching off; 7. A sergeant in charge as the platoon marches off; 8. Lieut. D.G. Howell with a platoon.

Tom Jones. A Cheltenham member of the Home Guard and an air raid precautions warden, Tom Jones worked throughout the war as a carpenter and joiner at S.C. Morris and Sons in Tivoli.

Albert Henry Smith. Another proud member of the Home Guard, Albert Smith lived at Savona in Oakland Avenue. During the war he worked for the GWR as a railway inspector; previously he had been a Baptist minister in Gloucester.

Vic Pulsford. A member of the removal company family, Vic Pulsford poses with his wife Nell (on the left) and his daughter Jean aged seven (in front). The girl on the right was a lodger called Joy: she was the first woman manager of Cheltenham's Marks and Spencer.

Ammunition training. Members of the Home Guard were trained in August 1941 in the use of Mills bomb projectors.

A composite photograph of Home Guard troops taking part in various exercises. Images of the Home Guard and their valiant and organized work were constantly published in the papers in order to sustain and build the morale of the public. 1. The Brockhampton Home Guard with Sergeant L.J. Thompson of Westwood Farm standing in the centre; 2. An ARP Mobile Squad and Home Guard dealing with 'casualties' following an exercise 'fight'; 3. Taking up firing positions – training in the event of an invasion.

Opposite below: Mock invasion. In February 1942 a full-scale mock invasion exercise was enacted in Cheltenham, complete with tanks. The following few pictures illustrate the exercise, and above all the good spirit that was alive.

Above: Dowty Home Guard. Men employed at Dowty's during the war created their own platoon for the factory – affectionately known as Dowty's Private Army. Cheltenham was granted the title of 1st Battalion of the Home Guard that wore the Gloucestershire Regimental badge. Including Winchcombe, Smith's factory, Dowty's, Bristol Tramways and Tewkesbury, the battalion at its height had 1,844 members.

Home Guard in the Promenade. When Anthony Eden asked for volunteers for a domestic fighting force he warned that they would not be paid, but that they would get a uniform and be armed.

The Battle of Cheltenham. This was another title given to the mock invasion. Here members of the volunteer Auxiliary Fire Service get involved.

Defending the post office. In the Promenade this group of stalwart and determined men stand fast to defend the post office against any raiders. For the town-based platoons much of the field training was given in the municipal gardens.

Armed to the teeth! The rifles distributed were either ex-First World War rifles or .303s. As well as machine gun and rifle training the men were given anti-gas training.

Above: Warship Week. In November 1941 Cheltenham held a warship week (see also page 15). To commemorate the event there was a parade through the town of local sea cadets.

Left: José and Alfred Chapman. José Chapman was born in Charlton Kings, where she has now returned to live. She had a varied career in the war working in ENSA, the Land Army and ultimately as a Junior Commander in the Army. At the time of the photograph, taken at Upton St Leonards, she was working in the Land Army. Her father, a musician by trade, was a proud member of the Home Guard. (See also page 100.)

Opposite above: Land Army. Members of the Land Army at Cirencester Agricultural College. Second from left is Mrs J.L. Stephens of Two Hedges in Woodmancote.

Opposite below: Relaxing in the hay. After a hard day's work three members of the Land Army and two friends take a minute's break. Mrs J.L. Stephens is sitting in the centre. Land work was intense and varied: dairying, tractor driving, rat-catching and ditch-digging were among the tasks expected of the women.

Above: Women at War. Miss M.C. Stephens from Woodmancote poses in the centre on a Fordson ration truck. Her friends are Margaret Hart (on the left) and a man known as 'Ginger'. Taken while stationed at RAF Great Witcombe, the huts in the background were the living quarters they had to endure.

Left: Miss M.C Stephens. Seen here at RAF Worcester in 1942 on the Bedford truck she drove as an MT driver, Miss Stephens volunteered for the WRAF in December 1941. She served in the 81st Signals Wing, 26 Group, Bomber Command, until she was demobbed in February 1946.

Opposite below: Serviceman's wedding. On Saturday 24 February 1940 Private Edward Lionel Iles RASC married Miss Olive Jean Mary Macintyre at Cheltenham parish church. Private Iles had been manager of Sealey's Industries before his call-up, and his bride worked at Cavendish House.

Above: Christmas 1941. Miss Stephens was still a 'rookie' when she was given the afternoon off on Christmas Day from her post at RAF Innsworth. This family photograph taken at Two Hedges shows, left to right: Mrs Phyllis Griffin, Joan Stephens, Mr William Griffin, Mrs J.L. Stephens, Bertram Griffin, Miss Dorothy Stephens, Miss Lillian Straight, Mary (a friend of Miss Stephens, in the front), Mr Derek Waters (behind), Miss M.C. Stephens, Mrs Evelyn Waters.

Mobile library. Artillerymen stationed near Cheltenham were given the opportunity to select and borrow books from the YMCA mobile library that had been presented by Mrs J.H. Trye. At the time it was believed to be the biggest and best-equipped of the twelve mobile libraries operated by the YMCA.

YMCA hut. Servicemen are seen here relaxing inside the new extension to the YMCA huts at Lansdown, April 1942. (See also page 121.)

Leslie S. Smith of 63 Marle Hill Parade enlisted in the RAF on 17 May 1944. After his initial training he was sent to Singapore, where he saw out the war.

William Jones. Being a member of the militia before the war, Bill Jones was one of the first to be called up in 1939. Initially he was sent to Yeovil as a member of the Royal Service Corps, then later he was posted overseas and in 1941 went to Sudan. While home on leave on 14 December 1940 he took the opportunity to marry his sweetheart Mary – just two days after the home of his parents in Kipling Road had suffered bomb damage.

Above: Junior Commander José Chapman. Miss Chapman obtained her three pips and title of Junior Commander holding an administrative job in Leicester. She was released from duty on 14 May 1946 – but has never actually been discharged. She is shaking the paw of the dalmation while her colleague has a firm hold of the lead, as the dog was never relaxed in male company (the photographer was male!).

Left: J.T. Jones. While still in the Home Guard Jimmy Jones returned home on the night of 11 December 1940 during the air raid, made himself a hot drink and then heard and felt a bomb land outside his home in Kipling Road. Not a pane of glass was broken, but the whole house moved about 4½ inches off its foundations. Jimmy was called up in August 1941 to work as an aircraft electrician.

Above: Stationed overseas. Jimmy Jones, on the left, spent six months of his service working as an aircraft electrician on Spitfires; then he was sent to the Middle East for three and a half years, when he never touched an aircraft. Instead he used his training on motor vehicles and helped in the construction of what is now Cairo airport, where this photo was taken.

Right: Brothers reunited. On learning that his brother was also in the Middle East, Bill Jones requested and was given some leave to go from the Sudan to Cairo to see him. The brothers were reunited in December 1942 and spent some days together exploring Cairo and the pyramids. Bill is on the left, Jimmy on the right.

The ultimate sacrifice. Second from the right stands Sergeant Air Gunner Reginald Stephens from Charlton Kings on a Scottish railway station with colleagues following training in 1940. His Wellington bomber, part of 38 Squadron, was shot down over Berlin on 7 October 1940. He is buried at Charlottenberg Cemetery in Berlin.

Six

Visitors

Evacuated. A little unnamed girl from Dagenham who arrived at Bishops Cleeve station on Saturday 15 June. Surely the evacuated children who came from the Midlands and the Home Counties were among the worst victims of war—taken from their homes and sent to live with strangers in strange towns.

St Monica's Home children. In January 1940 these girls were given a party at 4 St Margaret's Terrace by staff of Messrs A.C. Fincken and Co., who had formed a social club. The girls were members of St Monica's Waifs and Strays Home and were staying at the hospital in Battledown, having moved from London.

Film star visit. On Tuesday 23 January 1940 film actor Graham Moffat—standing centre with a bow tie—visited the Gaumont Palace cinema to meet fans. Graham Moffat achieved a modicum of fame as a 'fat boy' in British films.

Right: Queen Mary. King George's mother visited Cheltenham on 5 August 1942. Here she is leaving the YMCA Royal Well Bed Centre, followed by Mayor T.W. Waite.

Below: YMCA funds. Queen Mary is receiving purses for YMCA funds. During the war the royal family travelled extensively around the country to try to keep morale high.

Opposite above: King George VI. On 19 July 1944 the king and queen visited Smith's Industries. Here the engineering director R. Lenoir shows the king some watch and clock products.

Opposite below: King George and Queen Elizabeth. During their visit to Smith's in July 1944, Queen Elizabeth shakes the hand of Sir Allan Gordon-Smith. Walking behind the queen is Sir Stafford Cripps, Minister of Aircraft Production, and second from the right is Ben Havilland.

Town Hall. Queen Mary posing with Mayor T.W. Waite inside the Town Hall during the Dig for Victory exhibition in April 1942.

Brunswick Street. The queen visited Brunswick Street on 5 August 1942 to witness the damage caused by Cheltenham's second worst air raid, which took place on 27 July 1942. In the raid eleven people were killed and twenty-seven injured in Cheltenham, much of the misery being centred on Brunswick Street. Directly behind the queen is the Revd W.R. Bellerby and Mayor T.W. Waite.

The Duchess of Gloucester. In April 1942 HRH the Duchess of Gloucester came to Cheltenham to witness the Dig for Victory exhibition. As a tribute to her the Home Guard lined up for an inspection.

Australian nurses. Among the many foreigners who came to the town during the war was this group of nurses from the Australian Army Nursing Service. They were entertained in August 1940 at Sandford Park Swimming Pool by Mayor John Howell and Mayoress Mrs Stewart Billings. Members of the WVS provided and helped with teas.

Norwegians. In June 1940 local farmers engaged a number of refugee Norwegian whalers, who had fled to Britain following Hitler's hostilities. Here they are pictured at the Cheltenham PA Institution with Judge Kennedy, Mr W.A. Shee and Matron.

Polish airmen. On Monday 5 August 1940 a group of Polish airmen stationed in the town gave a public performance to 1,400 people in the Town Hall. These are men of the chorus.

In costume. These airmen are in costume on the same occasion for the performance of the mazurka – a traditional Polish dance.

Even the circus came to town! Six elephants of the Bertram Mills Circus with an average age of seven years were paraded in front of the Town Hall on Monday 20 May 1940. They had come to drink the spa waters in the hope that it would cure their rheumatism: they each drank a bucketful.

Joe Louis. In April 1944, on a wartime tour for US troops, world heavyweight champion Joe Louis came to Cheltenham to give his first boxing display in England. At Reeves Field he gave an exhibition bout with his sparring partner Bob Smith. The spectacle was limited to American GIs and men in uniform—consequently many members of the local Home Guard managed to get in to watch, as did boy scouts.

Seven

Around the Town

The Promenade. The upper part of Cheltenham's Promenade as it looked at the beginning of the war. The Promenade was very highly regarded, and regularly patrolled by a policeman who would turn you away if you were improperly dressed.

The Promenade Café. The interior of the Gloucestershire Dairy Company's Promenade Café during the war. The appearance of the café's façade can be seen in the photograph above.

Snowed under. In January 1942 Cheltenham suffered a severe snowfall. Here men try to clear a passable route for pedestrians down the Promenade.

January 1942. Notice how it seems to be more important that the pavements are cleared of snow than the roads. Motor vehicles were still relatively rare in the town and most of them were delivery vehicles.

Promenade and gardens. Taken before the railings came down for re-use in the war effort, this photograph shows the Municipal Offices on the right and the Promenade and gardens on the left in 1939 or 1940.

Montpellier Walk and Rotunda. Of the same period as the photograph above, this shows the top end of the town. The Rotunda on the left was used as an ammunition store during the war.

Above and below: Removal of cannon. In April 1942 it was decided that the two cannons standing proudly outside the Queen's Hotel would be removed, and the metal would be salvaged for use in the war effort. The guns were captured by the British from the Russians at the Battle of Sebastopol in 1855, during the Crimean War.

Removal of railings. In February 1942 the railings surrounding the Queen's Hotel were removed—again so that the metal could be salvaged. Virtually all the railings in Cheltenham were taken down during the war with the intention of re-use, and yet many of them were never salvaged and instead merely dumped.

Roden House and Berkeley House. On Saturday 22 June 1940 the railings were removed from around the fronts of the homes of Brigadier-General and Mrs J.L.R. Gordon, who lived at Roden House, and Mrs Cowing, who lived at Berkeley House.

Above: Scrap Metal Week. Between 22 and 29 June 1940 a Scrap Metal Week was arranged, in which people were encouraged to sort out any metal that could be re-used and take it to one of the several dumps in the town. One of the largest dumps was at Francis Street.

Below: Pig food. On the corner of Hewlett Street and All Saints' Road was this pig bin, for the collection of vegetables and other waste table scraps. It was fervently believed during the war that absolutely nothing should be wasted.

Moving the tank. This First World War tank, which had stood proudly for many years in the Montpellier Gardens, was finally removed in June 1940 in order that it could be used (as the press recorded) for 'defence purposes'.

Coal reserve dump. Photographed in October 1940 is this 1,000-ton stack of coal in the town. Several reserve dumps were arranged by Mr G.G. Marsland, the local Fuel Controller, and were only to be used in emergency.

Montpellier Gardens. Mayor T.W. Waite opened the new British Restaurant in the Montpellier Gardens in June 1942. On the far right stands the ex-Mayor John Howell.

Lansdown. In April 1942 an extension was made to the YMCA hut at Lansdown. The huts were a great source of entertainment and relaxation, in particular for the troops who were stationed in the vicinity.

The Winter Gardens. After years of neglect and in a state of disrepair the Winter Gardens, which stood in the gardens between the Town Hall and the Queen's Hotel, were finally demolished in September 1940. This, one of the last photographs of the interior of the Winter Gardens, was taken after builders had already taken out the flooring.

Cheltenham Spa bowling green. On Saturday 27 April 1940 Mayor John Howell opened the 1940 bowling season by bowling the first wood. Mr D.L. Lipson MP, who was president of the club, welcomed the mayor and a match was played between the captain's and vice-captain's sides.

The Lilleybrook Hotel, Cirencester Road, Charlton Kings, 1940. The hotel recently changed its name to the Cheltenham Park Hotel.

Prestbury Park. This was the Broadway Novice's Chase at Cheltenham Races, on Wednesday 13 March 1940. Mrs M.A. Gemmell's 'Agleam' ridden by T.F. Carey leads the field two fences from home. Immediately behind are Mr J. Ismay's grey 'Vitement', ridden by D. Butchers, and on the right Mrs E.W.W. Bailey's 'Sir Bill', ridden by Mr E.W.W. Bailey. At the last fence 'Golden Knight' and 'Iceberg II' jumped together, but then Golden Knight swerved in the run-in and was disqualified. Lord Sefton's 'Iceberg II' was awarded the race, 'Sir Bill' came in second and Mr J.H. Witney's 'National Night' was third.

Albion Venturer. Although delivered in 1940 to Cheltenham District Bus Company, this new Albion Venturer, one of several purchased, had been produced to the relative luxury of pre-war specifications. This No. 29 is pictured at Lansdown station in April 1940. Note the masked headlamps, and white wings and skirts – necessary because of the blackout restrictions.

Black and White coach station. This No. 56 bus at the Black and White coach station illustrates the utility standards that wartime vehicles were produced to. They had very angular bodies with wooden slatted seats. As paint supplies ran short, later models were turned out in drab grey.